Make $1000 Selling on eBay Before Christmas

Table of Contents

Why you should read this book

Are your credit cards maxed out? Are you unsure where the money will come from to pay for Christmas presents this year? Is it doubtful that Santa will wiggle down your chimney this year? Do you need a way to make a few bucks fast?

This book can help you overcome all of those fears.

You're about to learn how to make $500 to $1000 selling on eBay before Christmas. Unlike other books you may have read, this book will be short and to the point. You only have a few weeks to put everything into motion, so we will take several short, simple baby steps to move you in the right direction.

I'm going to give you a plan you can follow over and over again to make money now – for Christmas and in the future whenever you find yourself strapped for a little cash.

———————

First, let me tell you what this isn't. It's not a get-rich-quick scheme where you can put in fifteen minutes and get $1000 in your mailbox the following day. It's more like a job with lots of overtime and hard work. But, if you follow the plan –

I promise you will make $500, or $1000, or even more before Christmas.

Why listen to me?

What makes me qualified to help you sell on eBay?

My name is Nick Vulich. I have been selling on eBay since 1999. Last month I sold over 300 old magazines that most people and libraries would have thrown away as worthless junk. In my better months before the recession hit back in 2008, I used to take in $5000, even $6000 a month.

According to eBay, I have completed nearly 40,000 transactions since November 2, 2001, for just over $600,000.

I think that makes me uniquely qualified to show you how to make a few bucks on eBay. I know what it's like trying to figure out just what you want to sell, and that's not anything – compared to figuring out how you will approach selling those same items.

It's scary. And it's that fear that keeps a lot of people from even trying to sell on eBay. I don't know how often I have shown people what I do, and they say – yeah! They understand. But they don't get it because they don't understand why people buy what I sell.

I know the ins and outs of eBay, and if you are ready, I can show you what you need to know to help you take that next step, where you can make $100 TODAY and every day you need it.

Getting started

eBay Account. The first thing you need is an eBay account.

The good news is – They're free, and you can sign up for one in less than five minutes. If you don't already have an eBay account, you can sign up for one now by visiting get started with eBay.

When you sign up, they ask for some simple information. First, they need to know your name and email address. Next, they ask you for a username. Your username is how people know you on eBay, so be sure to put some thought into it. If you know what you want to sell, it will make picking a username easier.

If your name is Nick, and your reason for selling on eBay is to get some cash for Christmas presents, you could try nickschristmascash.

If you can't come up with a good idea right now, don't sweat it, eBay lets you change your id every 30 days.

PayPal account. You're going to need a way to get paid. PayPal used to be the easiest way to get paid. Over the last year, eBay has rolled out its managed payments program. The process is seamless for buyers. They can pay using PayPal or a credit card. eBay takes a day or two to process the payment, then deposits the proceeds, less selling fees, into your bank account. You can also leave the money on account and use it to fund purchases on eBay.

_____

You will need a digital camera. Your cell phone camera will also work just fine. You will also want to have a postal scale and a ruler.

Finally, before you start, find a nice quiet spot to work where you can be free from all distractions.

What should you sell?

One of the hardest things for most people is figuring out what they want to sell on eBay.

It doesn't have to be that hard. Most people get started selling items they already have around the house. Look around you. You probably have some great things you're no longer using.

Do you have some shoes you don't wear anymore? Have you upgraded your old cell phone in the past year? If you have kids, did they outgrow any of their clothes? Remember that ugly sweater mom gave you for Christmas last year? Has anyone taken any college classes recently? Someone is going to need those textbooks.

Do you get the idea? We all have things sitting around the house we no longer use. But they're still great items, and the chances are pretty good there's somebody out there who'd be willing to pay a few bucks for them.

Most people don't get past this first step because they don't see the value in the things they have around them. You don't use landline phones anymore, but many people still do. You can drop it in the trash can, take it to Good Will, or maybe, just maybe – you can take a long hard look at it and see that phone as twenty-five bucks towards your Christmas wish list.

———————

Now I know there will be a few sour pusses who say they "got nothing." But like Charlie Brown at Halloween, they've got a bag full of rocks.

Suppose there really is nothing in your house you can sell. How will you get that $1000 you need to play Santa this year?

It can be as easy as going to the store. Several Christmases ago, my wife was shopping at Jo Ann Fabrics and came across Bedazzler's discounted to five bucks. She had been looking at them on eBay, and they were selling for $80 to $100, so when she got home, the first thing she did was check eBay. They were still selling for $80 to $100. She compared her Bedazzler to those selling on eBay, and sure enough – they were the same. The eBay sellers didn't have any "magic Bedazzlers." They were just getting a whole lot more money for the ones they had.

To make a long story short, we bought every Bedazzler Jo Ann Fabric and all of the ones available from every JoAnn's within fifty miles.

I sold 87 Bedazzlers for $50 to $75 over six weeks. I probably could have gotten more money for them, but I unloaded them too quickly and flooded the market.

This Thanksgiving, I picked up two PlayStation 5 game consoles at Walmart for $569 each. I could easily turn them around on eBay for $750 to $800 each for a quick score, but then the kids would be disappointed.

———————

Walmart, Target, T J Maxx, and other local stores are excellent sources for items to sell on eBay.

These big stores are all about moving large quantities of items. When sales slow down or the season changes, they're ready to move on to the latest thing. So, what happens to the old items? They mark them down and move them to the clearance section.

Most of these items are still new. However, other stores across the country are still selling them at full price, so if you can get them at a bargain price, you can resell them for a tidy profit on eBay.

In 2001, I stopped at a Big Lots store in West Virginia. They had several Starting Lineup Basketball Headliner sets they were closing out for twenty bucks each. The regular price was $100. What made these items special was that they had a Michael Jackson figure. To make a long story short, I bought all five sets they had left and resold them for $85 each.

We have a Shoe Carnival store in town. We used to go in and pick out ten pairs of boots or shoes every week that they had marked down to ten or fifteen dollars. Most of them sold within a week or two for at least twice what we paid. The ones we had trouble selling, we marked down to what we paid for them and moved on to something else.

You can do the same thing in your town. This works especially well in cities with large outlet malls or stores like JC Penney, Nike, or Sears. You could easily pick out five or ten items to sell on every visit.

If you're unsure which items will sell the best, bring along your iPhone or Android and check the going price on Amazon or eBay.

———————

I visit used bookstores in my spare time, looking for new items I can sell. Last summer, I discovered three county history books from the late 1800s. I got them for $100 to $125 each. I sold all three on eBay for $250 to $400 each within two weeks.

Estate sales have loads of great stuff waiting for you to discover. Local auctions offer the same opportunity. Remember to wear your "money vision" goggles when visiting these places. You will be amazed at the great things you've been walking by for your entire life.

It doesn't take a lot of time or effort to find stuff to sell. You just have to really look at the things around you. Profitable items are everywhere.

———————

Now that we've picked out what we're going to sell, the next section will go into the nitty-gritty of how to sell them. This is important to you because eBay has millions of sellers, and they are all competing with you to get the buyer's attention.

Luckily for you, most sellers have no idea what they have or how to sell it.

Let me repeat what I said in the last chapter.

Most sellers have no idea what they have or how to sell it ...

What's the secret to selling your item for the most money possible?

It's easy...

Put yourself in your buyer's shoes. Take a minute to think about why they want what you're selling. Who is the ideal customer for it? Why would anyone want your old Kindle? What can they do with it? What could they do with it? Most people never think of using it for more than reading. Did you?

I suggest considering how an item can be used and picking out five or six to sell your buyer.

In the case of the Kindle, obviously, you can use it to read e-books. Most sellers are going to leave it at that. It's easy. They don't have to put a whole lot of thought into it. Shoot a picture. Say I've got a Kindle Fire. Give me a hundred bucks.

Unfortunately, your poor Kindle Fire will be lost in the crowd if you do the same things everyone else does. A quick search shows 1208 of them on sale today.

Let's try to up the odds of selling our Kindle. What if we said our Kindle was also a great internet tablet; you can download and watch movies on the go; it's great for email; you can download music and listen to it with your earbuds. Maybe we could say it's the poor man's I-pad?

It doesn't really matter what you're selling. You need to think outside the box when listing items on eBay.

My thing is old books and magazines. Every day old volumes of Harper's Magazine from the 1850s to the early 1900s come up for sale on eBay. Most of the time, sellers list them for ten to fifteen dollars. Most sellers post a picture of the dilapidated old leather cover falling apart and say it's an old book in poor condition. Very few of them open the book up to look at all the great woodcut illustrations. Why not show a few of these? Maybe you can list some of the contents? It will take some extra time, but the odds are that the time you spend attending to these details can be the difference between selling your book for $10 or $50.

Let me give you an example.

There is a bookseller I've been following on eBay for five or six years now. He sells the same books everyone else sells for $10 to $25. The only difference is that he receives dozens of bids and often sells the same book for $100 to $200.

Any guesses why he receives so much more money for his books?

He puts in the extra time to craft a great description. He tells people what the book is about. He shares passages from it. And he isn't stingy with pictures. Many of his listings have twenty or more images in them. Sure, you can say a book has great illustrations. But a photo will show buyers exactly how great those illustrations are.

With all that being said, what's the perfect description?

Write the best description for each item. Don't worry about how long it takes. Instead, worry about what potential buyers need to know. Many items can be described in fifty or a hundred words, but some items may take four hundred to five hundred words to properly describe.

Time to start selling

You first need to know that selling on eBay isn't free. It's going to cost you a little money. The nice thing about eBay is you don't have to pay your fees when you list your item. Instead, they collect the payment from your buyer and deduct any selling fees from the proceeds. Then, your share is deposited in your bank account a few days later.

As an eBay member without an eBay Store, eBay gives you an extra bonus for selling.

Your first fifty auction-style or fixed-price listings are FREE. After that, you only have to pay final value fees if your item sells.

Used properly and combined with your great items, this should be more than enough opportunities to make some extra cash.

About eBay fees. Depending upon what you are selling, eBay will hit you with a 9% to 14% final value fee when your item sells. It's part of the cost of doing business. Consider it your rent. If you have a store, you have to pay the landlord. You have to pay for the ad if you list your stuff in the paper. You must pay for your booth if you sell at a flea market. eBay is no different. You have to pay to play.

eBay is where people gather to check out and buy other people's junk. If you're not there, you're not going to see that extra money you need for Christmas shopping.

Different Ways to Sell

There are several different ways to sell your items on eBay. The three primary listing types are 1) Auction, 2) Fixed Price, and 3) Classified.

Of the three, auction and fixed price are what you will be using most.

Auction listings allow potential buyers to bid against each other for your item, much as they would attending a local auction. The way it works is – bidders place what is called a "proxy bid." When they do this, they tell eBay that they are willing to spend up to a certain amount, $10.00, $15.00, whatever they set as their upper bid limit. From here, eBay places your bid for you up to your maximum bid. For example, suppose the seller starts her auction at $9.99, and your "proxy bid" is $25.00. In that case, eBay will place your bid for $9.99, the seller's minimum acceptable bid. If someone else places a bid, they will advance yours up to your $25.00 limit.

Fixed price listings are like walking into your local Walmart or Best Buy. You see a price on the shelf, and that is the price you have to pay. There is no bargaining, finagling, or whatever. Whoever agrees to pay the asking price gets the item.

Classified Listings are more informational. They are a way for businesses to get information out there about what they are doing. An example would be someone selling eBay training seminars. They can give information about their offering and give you an email address or phone number to follow up with for more information (something not allowed in an auction or fixed price listings).

eBay also offers variations on the above listings that everyone should consider using. The most important of these tools is **Buy-It-Now**. Adding buy-it-now to your auction listing allows you to start your item at a low price yet reach for the sky. If someone exercises the buy-it-now option, the auction ends, and the bidder wins the item. If, on the other hand, someone makes the minimum bid, the buy-it-now option disappears, and the only way to buy the article is by bidding on it.

I use buy-it-now to set my starting price at the lowest price I am willing to accept. Then I put my buy-it-now price at three or four times my starting price. It's the price I would ideally like to receive.

Best offer is another spin eBay offers for fixed-price auctions. Best offer is just like it sounds. You price the item, and potential buyers can buy your item at a fixed price, or they can send you an offer. Be prepared to laugh a little and cry a little at some of the offers you receive. I had a guy one day who made a $1.00

offer on fifty different items I was selling for $25.00 each. You would think he would have better things to spend his time on.

I've found that most people will offer you between one-half and two-thirds of your asking price. On the other hand, some will continuously lowball you at $5.00, and others will thank you profusely for just taking a few bucks off the price.

The good news is: eBay lets you totally automate the process. When you set up the best offer option, you can tell eBay to accept offers over such, and such a price and decline offers below a specific price. This way, you don't see any of those lowball offers. The only offers eBay will send to you are the ones that come in between your decline price and your accept price, so you can manually decide on them.

For example, if I set my accept price at $17.00 and my decline price at $10.00, eBay accepts all offers I receive over $17.00. If an offer comes under $10.00, they don't bother me. But suppose someone makes an offer between $10.00 and $17.00. In that case, they send a message to the person making an offer that the seller "is considering their offer." Then it's up to me. I can accept their offer. I can send a counteroffer And, we can bargain back and forth like this for another three tries.

Your first listing

This section will tell you everything you need to know to make your first sale on eBay. When you are done reading it, you will know how to write a compelling title that will bring hundreds of potential buyers to your listings. How to write a description that will leave them drooling for more, and how to shoot pictures that sell.

To start selling, click **sell** at the top of the eBay page, or visit the <u>Tell us what you want to sell page</u>.

If your item has a UPC or ISBN, enter it when prompted. If you don't have one of these or if you have a unique item, select browse categories. This will let you choose a category to list your item in. If you have an older book without an ISBN, choose fiction or non-fiction, and drill down into the category that best describes your book. For example, if you're selling a woman's leather jacket, select *women's clothing >> coats and jackets*.

How to write a compelling title

eBay gives you 80 characters to describe your item. So, the more information you can put into it, the more people will see your article.

Why? Because different things are important to different people. Some people search for iPods, and others search for iPods 8 GB. Still, others will be more interested in "certified," others for "Apple certified." If you want to buy on the cheap but still get something good, you may want "refurbished."

Let's look at a few titles on eBay for the iPod Touch...

.Apple iPod Touch 4th Generation Black 8GB (Used)

.Apple iPod Touch 32 GB Black (4th Generation) Apple Certified Refurbished

.Great Condition!!! No reserve. Apple iPod Touch 4th Generation Black 32 GB

.Apple iPod Touch 4th Generation 8GB – MC55OLL- works great-camera-earphone

.Apple iPod Touch 4th Generation 16GB New in Factory Sealed Box

Ok. Let's take a close look at those titles.

They're loaded with keyword-rich details.

.8GB, 16 GB, 32 GB

.black / white

.3rd generation / 4th generation

.Apple iPod Touch

.iPod touch

.factory sealed in box

. Apple Certified Refurbished

.camera

.earphone

Are you starting to get the idea?

Yeah! It's an iPod, but that's really the smallest part of it. It's all in the details. People really want an iPod Touch with one or all of the above features. If your title doesn't include the keywords a buyer is looking for, he will move on to the following listing.

Your job is to entice searchers to stop and look at your listing.

Let's look at another item

Nike Shoes.

If you type "Nike men's shoes" in the eBay search box, there are 219,158 pairs listed. That's like getting caught in rush hour traffic on the Eisenhower. Your shoes aren't going anywhere.

Without more details, your poor shoes will be lost in the rush.

What we need to do is level the playing field. You must consider what's important to people when they're looking for a new pair of shoes.

Some of the things they're going to look for are:

.size

.color

.athletic, loafer, dress, work boot

.width (d, ee)

.model number

.new / used

.new in box

.easy returns

.men's / women's / children's

How many of these terms describe the shoes, you are selling? If you want to sell those shoes, you need to fit as many of these keywords as you can in the 88 characters eBay allows you for a title. You will reduce your chances of making a sale if you miss just one.

A search on the following keywords (men's Nikes 10 ee new in box) reduced the number of pairs shown from 219,158 to six.

Obviously, you have a better chance of selling those shoes when you're one of six pairs rather than one of several hundred thousand.

Remember, your title doesn't have to be a complete sentence. It doesn't even have to make sense when you read it. It just needs to have enough keywords, so people can easily find your listing.

The takeaway here is to laser-focus your title. If you're unsure which keywords should be in your title, search eBay to see what keywords other sellers use. You can also peek at the manufacturers selling page to see how they describe the item.

Picture it sold...

You've heard the saying, "a picture is worth a thousand words." On eBay, the expression is a good picture is worth a thousand dollars.

You can have the best title, a great description, and a killer price, but if your pictures suck, you will have trouble closing the deal.

When people are ready to buy something, especially expensive items, they demand great pictures. The best example you can find here is your local car dealer. They don't stop with one image. You will often find twenty to twenty-five pictures for every car they sell. Your car dealer knows most customers shop online before they come in.

As a result, dealers give you a virtual tour of the car with the pictures they take. On the outside, they show you the front, back, and sides. In addition, there is at least one picture of the engine, a view into the trunk, the upper dashboard, the odometer showing the mileage, the floor – front and back, and close-ups of any damage.

You can learn a lot about the type of pictures you need by studying car dealers' listings. The lighting is always perfect. Every photo is perfectly centered. They never put in a lousy shot. They know one bad picture can kill the whole deal.

Plan your pictures the same way. You want at least one overall view of your item. You also want detailed close-up photos of any designs. If there is damage – don't just say it in the description; make sure to include one or two pictures of the affected area. Let potential buyers decide for themselves how bad the damage is.

eBay lets you upload 12 free pictures with every listing. Include as many as you need to tell your story.

———————————

eBay requires all photos to be a least 500 pixels on the longest end. 1600 pixels is suggested for the best results.

How do you resize your pictures?

If you are only running a few auctions, you can manually resize them in MS Paint. Open your pictures in Paint, use the resize tool, and save them. In my case, I usually scan 150 to 200 photos a day, and resizing them all manually would probably drive me over the edge. I use Adobe LightRoom. It lets me import all of my pictures with the click of a button, optimize them with two or three mouse clicks, and export them back to my desktop, all in less than five minutes.

Get as many pictures as you need to sell your item. Then, if the lighting is off or the image is off-center – retake it. A few extra minutes redoing it will pay significant dividends when you make the sale.

How to write a description that sells

Your item description is your sales pitch. The more useful information you can share about your item, the better your chances are of selling it at a premium price.

First and foremost, you need to be honest.

While writing about your item's great features, you must mention any defects. The last thing you want to do is make a sale and have it blow up in your face because of a scratch or any other minor blemish. Most people aren't worried about minor flaws or defects as long as they know about them when making the purchase. What bothers people is finding out about problems after they've laid down their hard-earned money.

What makes a great description?

Let's look at a few, and you will better understand how to craft a winning description every time.

_____

Up for auction is a rare US Senate document of Dubuque, Iowa historical interest, a March 30, 1846 report, 26 pages long, detailing the findings of the Committee on Private Land Claims regarding the claims of Julien Dubuque and August Chouteau and their heirs to "a tract of one hundred and forty-eight thousand... arpens of land, situate on the river Mississippi, at a place called the Spanish Mines, about four hundred and forty miles from St. Louis." After the Louisiana Purchase, the US government had to determine the validity of various French and Spanish land claims. In the document, the history of Dubuque and Chouteau's claim to the land, including their purchase of the land from the "Sac and Fox Nation of Indians" in 1788. Detailed discussion within about the claim's validity, the validity of the sale by the tribes, and much more. Today, this area contains the city of Dubuque, Iowa. A fascinating document. Originally bound into a larger bound volume of Senate reports, but discovered as such, and in total, a self-contained work of its own. The binding is still holding. Quite rare. Good luck!

———————

This auction is for a like-new condition Field Gear thick supple leather with super soft Genuine Raccoon Tail. Zip, removable hood. Jacket parka tag size is missing but fits like a man's large or extra-large. Please see the measurements to determine the best fit. This jacket is great, with no flaws, and looks barely worn! This jacket would make a great gift, or wear it yourself and impress your friends and family. Get this jacket in time for the upcoming fall and winter to look good and stay warm! Make this yours now, and please check out my store.

Measures shoulder to shoulder 21 inches, pit to pit 25 inches, top of shoulder to bottom 33 inches, and cuff to top of shoulder 24 inches.

———————

It is that time of year again. Wintertime. We are now starting to bring out our high-end winter clothing. We have over 300 Northface, Spyder, Pendleton, Patagonia, and many other high-end clothing pieces. So, please keep checking back because we will be putting up many things in the next three months. I also have a lot of winter boots available.

Up for sale is a men's Columbia heavy-duty jacket in size XL. Great anorak pullover jacket. Full side zipper. Super good-looking and warm. If you know *quality, then you know Columbia is the finest clothing out there. This is the same brand that my family wears. Super high-end and expensive. You will look fantastic in this clothing. It will keep you warm and dry.*

———————————

Tell a story – Make a sale

Each seller is telling a story and building value into their items.

The first one on the document tells you in a short, concise description of what you can expect to find in it, why it is important, and what condition it is in.

The two clothing items build on emotion. "This is the same brand my family wears." "Impress your friends and family." "You will look fantastic in this clothing."

The first clothing item also gives you exact measurements. That way, there is no guessing. Anyone who orders can be sure the coat will fit them.

Another takeaway from the last item is the pitch to look at their other items. "Be sure to keep checking back...I also have a lot of winter boots available."

You should refer to these listings when you start writing your description. You want to include specific details about the item you are selling – size, color, brand, and any defects. If you can – appeal to any emotions – "look great," "feel good," "be the envy of your friends and neighbors." People are drawn to items they like, but any car salesperson can tell you – emotion closes more sales than anything else.

Finally, if you are selling complimentary products, for example, jackets and pants or a series of books or movies – ask your buyers to check out your other auctions.

Price your items to sell

You've done it.

You've written a killer title loaded with keywords. Your description has left potential customers drooling over your item. It tells everything a buyer needs to make an informed decision, and it appeals to their emotions

Now all you've got to do is price your item right.

More sales are lost at this step than anywhere else in the sales process. This is because, too, often, sellers become overly attached to their items. Especially if it is an item, they've owned since childhood or one with a family history.

You see it on every episode of Pawn Stars. Rick or Cory call in an expert to appraise an item, and the expert appraises it at $1000. Yet the owner stubbornly holds on to their idea that because the item is old or has sentimental value, or they have this much money into it, they need a specific price for it, often times $500 or $1000 more than the expert appraised it at.

Bad idea. An item is only worth what someone is willing to pay for it.

Sometimes this fact works in your favor. Other times you have to shrug your shoulders and take what you can get.

In my case, I sell old magazine articles that have no set value. There is no official price, so I've learned to wing it and set my prices by experimenting with where they sell best. I know from past experience what topics will sell for more money or sell quicker. So, on those items, I jump my price by twenty or thirty dollars, and many times I can get it. If they don't sell, I drop the price and take what I can get.

A lot of items don't allow you this luxury. They sell day in and day out in a very narrow price range, and if you jump out of that price range – No sale.

———————

Here's one of the best ways to set your price to assure a quick sell-through, especially if you are a new seller.

You can do a completed item search on eBay using the advanced search feature.

To do a completed item search, find the search box at the top of the eBay page. To the right of the words **SEARCH,** it will say **ADVANCED**. Click on **ADVANCED**, which will take you to another set of search options.

Enter the keywords you want to search on. You can search in just one category or listings in all categories (I would recommend this one). A little further down, where it says **search including** be sure to check off by **completed listings**. As you scroll down, you will see many more options you can search by. Unless you are looking for some really specialized information, I would consider only Auction and Buy It Now under the Selling Formats category.

A quick look through completed listings for the last week will give you a good idea of the price range your item has sold in. You can drill down even more by clicking on the listings that sold for the most money and gathered the most bids.

Take a close look at the keywords sellers used in the title; what they said in the description; the type and number of pictures they included; and finally, the listing starting price. No use reinventing the wheel. Write all of this down; you can include much of it when you post your own listings.

This way, you can see exactly what items like yours have sold for. If enough items have sold, you will have an excellent idea of how much your item should sell for.

———————

There are several pricing theories.

One popular pricing strategy is to start every item at 99 cents and let the market determine the price. This works well with things that sell in large quantities and typically sell within a tight price range. Electronics are an excellent example of where this strategy can work for you. There are always plenty of buyers ready to pounce on an iPad, iPhone, or laptop. So, starting your item at 1 cent or 99 cents will spark a bidding war and bring you the best possible price.

Most people prefer knowing their item will bring at least a certain price. If you're selling an item that typically brings $100 to $125, maybe you can price it at $85 and add a Buy-It-Now option for $125. This guarantees a minimum price if your item sells while giving you a shot at getting the best price if someone exercises your Buy-It-Now.

Whatever you do, think hard before using the 99-cent strategy if you sell collectibles or one-of-a-kind items. Often a collectible, no matter how rare, only has one buyer at any time. So, if you can't spark a bidding war, that $100 or $500 item could sell for 99 cents.

Shipping your item

The biggest thing to remember about shipping is that you are responsible for the item until the seller receives it.

If your package gets lost in the mail, you must make good on it. If it arrives damaged, you need to make good on it. If your shipment arrives incomplete, and the buyer says all the pieces aren't there, you need to make good on it.

You need to package your item correctly. If you sell plates, glassware, or other fragile items, you must pack them, so they arrive undamaged. If you mail photos or articles that can be easily bent or folded, you need to package them in a sturdy mailer and mark "Do not bend or fold" all over the package. I don't know about your mail person, but my mail lady likes to bend and fold everything so she can cram it into my tiny mailbox.

Take a few moments before you list your item to think about how you will mail it. Will your item fit in a small box or card stock mailer? Or will you require lots of elaborate packing materials and sturdy corrugated boxes? What you sell will affect how you ship your item and what you charge for shipping.

eBay allows you several ways to charge shipping fees. You can choose a flat rate, where everyone pays the same shipping charge no matter where they live. For example, with this method, if you set your shipping fee at $5.00, everyone would pay $5.00, whether they live in the same state as you or 2,000 miles away in Alaska or Hawaii. You can also choose "calculated shipping." With calculated shipping, you enter the weight of your item when you list it, and eBay automatically computes shipping charges to any destination. Using calculated shipping, someone closer to you usually pays less for shipping, making your item more attractive to them.

eBay also lets you choose several methods of shipping. For example, you can offer first class, media, priority, or express mail. By providing choices, buyers can elect a less expensive shipping method or a more expensive one that will get their item to them quicker.

Another obstacle you will bump up against is Free Shipping. eBay wants everyone to offer free shipping. Their thought is you should absorb shipping and handling fees into your prices. My suggestion is to see what other sellers are doing with similar items.

You should probably join the pack if everyone else is offering free shipping. Otherwise, I would suggest charging separately for shipping.

———————

eBay makes it easy for you to mail your items.

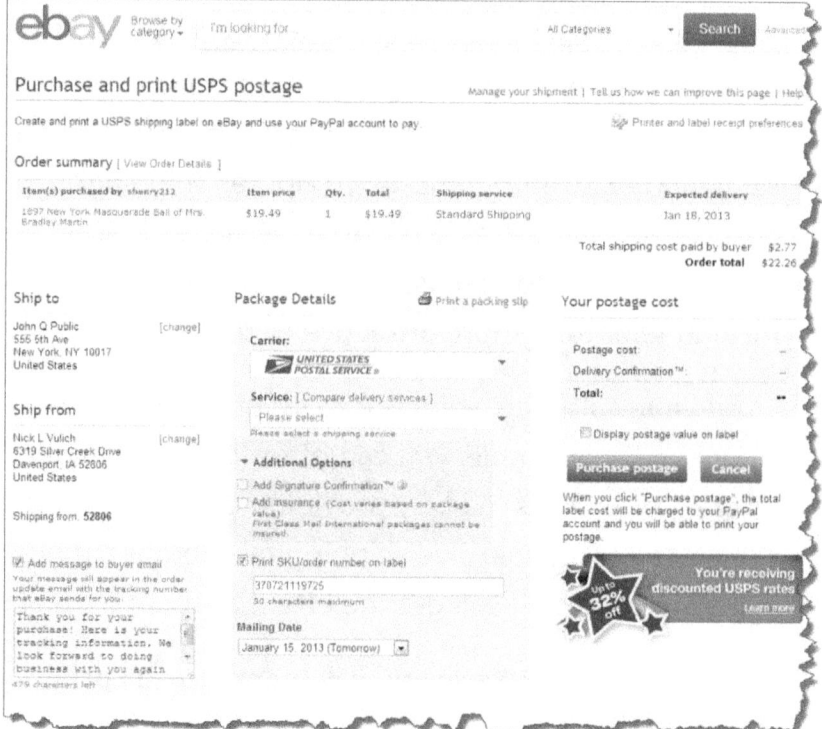

You can print shipping labels directly from the item listing as soon as your buyer pays. To do this, click **My eBay** at the top of the page. Select **Sold**

items in your selling manager. From here, go to the thing you need to mail and click in the final column where it says sell similar. From the drop-down menu, select **print shipping labels**. You will be taken to the Print a shipping label page.

Fill in the weight and shipping method if they aren't already prepopulated for you. From there, selecting the options you want is just a simple matter. For example, you can add delivery confirmation, signature confirmation, and insurance.

I want to take a minute and define those last three terms:

Delivery confirmation means the mailman scans your package when he leaves it at your customer's house. It is proof your item was delivered. If you print your mailing label through eBay or PayPal, delivery confirmation is included with most options. If you mail your item at the Post Office, you must fill out a special form and pay the fee ($1.05 at this writing).

You want to include delivery confirmation with every item you sell. It keeps you and your buyer honest. The first thing eBay or PayPal will do if the buyer starts an *item not delivered* case is check delivery confirmation. If it shows delivered – you win. If there's no delivery confirmation, you lose because there is no way to prove your item was ever shipped, let alone delivered.

Signature confirmation is similar to delivery confirmation, except the buyer must sign for your package to receive it. eBay and PayPal require signature confirmation on orders valued at over $200. You can include it with the label you print online. Once again, if you do your shipping at the Post Office, you must fill out a separate form.

Insurance is an extra you can add to most packages. Insurance pays for damage or loss of your items while in transit. You don't have to purchase insurance. It is an option. You need to remember that the seller is responsible for an item until it is delivered to the buyer in the condition you offered it for sale. You are responsible if the item does not arrive or arrives damaged.

Another thing to remember is eBay does not allow sellers to charge buyers for insurance. You can build it into your shipping cost or the price of your item. However, you cannot charge for it as a standalone option.

The takeaway here is to carefully pack and ship every item you sell. Then, select the shipping options and extras that are important to you. If you decide not to insure every package, pick a price point - $50 or $100 - that you will buy insurance at and stick to that. This way, you can limit your losses in case something unfortunate happens.

Another problem sellers face is that shipping costs go up during the holiday season. Most shippers add a surcharge to hire extra help during the holiday rush. I sell small items (under 8 ounces), and the increase costs me roughly forty cents per item. If you sell heavier stuff, it will cost you even more.

Most of the surcharges are in effect from late October through the first week of January. Check your carrier's web page for more details.

The USPS has gone even further. They've increased rates while slowing their services down. Unfortunately, that means customers will have to wait longer for their packages. So, you might want to warn them in your listings.

And finally, prepare for a USPS price increase in January. The holiday surcharges fall off, but the prices go up anyway.

Customer Service is everything

On eBay, the only thing a seller has is their good reputation.

Every time you sell an item, the buyer has the opportunity to leave feedback on how well they felt you handled the transaction. In addition, they can leave a written comment on what they thought of your service and product. Buyers can also rate you in four categories: item description, communication, how quickly you shipped their item, and cost of shipping.

It's called a five-star rating system because it can give you one to five stars in each category.

You would think getting four stars would be great, and it would be in an ideal system, but in the eBay world, four out of five stars can get you thrown off the site for poor customer service. eBay considers 4.8 to 5.0 as excellent customer service. Anything below 4.6 is deemed unsatisfactory, and you can lose your selling privileges.

So how do you give good customer service on eBay?

It all starts with your listing. You need to accurately describe all of your items. If there are flaws, you need to describe them completely and add photographs where possible.

Don't overcharge for shipping. Shipping charges are a really touchy issue on eBay right now. Even a hint of overcharging your customers can draw negative feedback in all four categories.

Answer your email promptly – within 24 hours, sooner if possible. If someone asks questions before or after the sale, respond immediately.

Promptly respond to complaints. Apologize profusely. Accept all blame for the problem, even if it's clear you're not at fault. When someone writes me because they haven't received their item yet, even if they just paid two days ago, and its shipping to Japan, I start my email with:

"I'm sorry to hear you haven't received your item yet. I did check my records. Your payment was received on ----, and it was mailed on ---. Normal delivery time is ------, so you should receive your item soon. Please keep me advised. Nick"

Notice – I don't go off on them for expecting the impossible. I apologize. I tell them the facts –

when they paid and when their item was mailed. And finally, I set expectations for delivery time. I end by telling them it's ok to keep in touch.

Show concern. That's really all most people want.

What about requests for refunds? One of my first jobs was with Radio Shack, and every time we had to give out a refund, the manager would head for the back room as soon as the customer left and start screaming and ranting. Often times he would smash the returned item, crashing it into the wall or the floor. I mention this only to point out how not to handle the situation.

Your reputation is at stake when you sell online, and someone wants a refund. The best thing you can do is apologize. Offer a full refund, including shipping both ways. The only alternative is facing the likelihood of receiving negative feedback. In the long run, that will cost you more than any refund you give.

Time to get started...

Ok. We've covered how to find items to sell. How to list your items and price them for a quick sale.

Christmas is just a few weeks away, and it's time to get your rear in gear. The only thing keeping you from making this your best Christmas ever is fear of trying.

I know you can do it. Every day thousands of people just like you get started selling on eBay. Thousands more want to try it but are afraid to try. Don't be one of them.

Happy Holidays, and great selling.

Nick

1) **Start your prices low**.

No matter what pricing strategy you use – whether you start all of your auctions at 99 cents or at a higher price, try to undercut your competition by at least 10 percent.

2) **If you're selling auction style, include Buy-it-now.**

Most people will pay a premium price to quickly get the item they want. Always include a buy-it-now price, and make it a stretch from your regular price. Five to ten dollars extra is good. I've often started my item at $9.99 and added a $159.99 buy-it-now. A lot of times, I've got it.

3) **If you sell with a fixed price, include best offer**.

People like to feel they're getting a deal. Sure, many people will lowball you, but just as many will offer a fair price. So, give it a shot, and your sales will go up.

4) **Offer a combined shipping discount**.

Knock a couple dollars off of shipping for each additional item your customer purchases. Better yet, offer to ship any additional purchases at no extra charge. A lot of customers will take you up on the deal.

5) **Use eBay to ship your stuff.**

Printing your shipping label through eBay transfers the shipping information, so you don't have to worry about typing in the wrong address. In addition, delivery confirmation is automatically included with most shipping options. Finally, tracking information is updated on the item listing so customers can check it whenever they like.

6) **Offer a Money Back Guarantee**.

A money-back guarantee makes your customer feel good about shopping with you. It's the internet, after all, and people are buying from you sight unseen. It's a little scary, even if you always purchase items online.

One of the first things I did when I started selling full-time was to offer my customers a 100 % Money Back Guarantee.

"Here at history-bytes, we understand that buying an item online can sometimes be a little scary. For that reason, we offer a 100 % Money Back Guarantee. If you are unhappy for any reason, we will refund your money – No questions asked."

One of the main reasons sellers give for not offering refunds is they're afraid they will constantly be giving people their money back. I can tell you that is not an issue. I've made ten refunds in fourteen years of selling, with over 40,000 items sold. There is always going to be someone who is going to take advantage of you. It happens. Don't let your fear about that one person stop you from offering refunds.

7) **Offer gift wrapping or include a card**.

Make it easy for customers to buy from you. For example, offer to gift wrap your item or enclose a Christmas card. A little extra work can score a lot of additional sales for the holidays.

8) **Include a short video**.

If you sell remote control toys or something that lends itself to video, include a video of your item in action. Another idea is to have a short video about your item, how to use it, or how carefully you package it.

9) **Focus on the positive**.

Many sellers waste time saying all the things they won't do, or they list a whole bunch of policies that make people want to click out of their item descriptions. My advice is to focus on the positive. Tell people what you will do, not what you won't do.

10) **Offer international shipping**.

A lot of sellers freak out over international shipping, but it's really no harder to ship internationally than it is in the United States.

eBay's Global Shipping Program was revamped in 2022 and simplifies international shipping. You can opt into it when listing your item for sale.

It doesn't get any easier. You ship your item to one of eBay's shipping providers in the United States, and from there on out, they do all of the work and are responsible for delivery. You don't need to fill out any customs forms or anything. Just sit back and watch the extra sales roll in.

www.ingramcontent.com/pod-product-compliance
Lightning Source LLC
Chambersburg PA
CBHW051224170526
45166CB00005B/2026